BEAMISH
40 YEARS ON RAILS
Railways, Tramways, and Waggon Ways

Roger R Darsley & Paul D Jarman
Series editor   Vic Mitchell

MP Middleton Press

Front cover upper: 2010 and Beamish is a very busy station after the restoration of passenger services on the railway.(P.D.Jarman)

Front cover lower: 1970 and the first building to be brought to the museum was Rowley station on the Stanhope & Tyne Railway. Opened in 1867 it was the first station west of Consett. The station was carefully dismantled to be rebuilt on the museum site and renamed Beamish. (D.Davis/Beamish coll.)

Rear cover upper: Night time in Beamish Town with a line-up of trams in 2005 to launch a sponsorship scheme. On the right is Sunderland no.16 and behind it is Gateshead no.10. On the other line is Sheffield no.264 and hiding behind it is Newcastle no.114. (P.D.Jarman)

Rear cover lower. A line-up of the replicas Puffing Billy, Steam Elephant, *and* Locomotion *stand outside the Great Shed (P.D.Jarman)*

Visiting Beamish

Readers intending to visit Beamish are advised to consult www.beamish.org.uk to check opening times and for details of special events. Alternatively please telephone 0191 370 4000.

Summer Season
Easter to the end of October
Open every day from 10am to 5pm, last admission 3pm.

Winter Season
November through to Easter of the following year
Open 10am to 4pm, last admission 3pm.

A winter visit is centred on The Town, Pit Village and Tramway only. Other areas of the Museum are closed and admission charges are, consequently, reduced.

Transport news and updated stocklists can be found (and downloaded) from the curator's blog at http://beamishtransport.blogspot.com

---

Published March 2011

ISBN 978 1 906008 94 9

© Middleton Press, 2011

Design Deborah Esher

Published by
> *Middleton Press*
> *Easebourne Lane*
> *Midhurst*
> *West Sussex*
> *GU29 9AZ*

Tel: 01730 813169
Fax: 01730 812601
Email: info@middletonpress.co.uk
www.middletonpress.co.uk

Printed in the United Kingdom by Henry Ling Limited, at the Dorset Press, Dorchester, DT1 1HD

CONTENTS

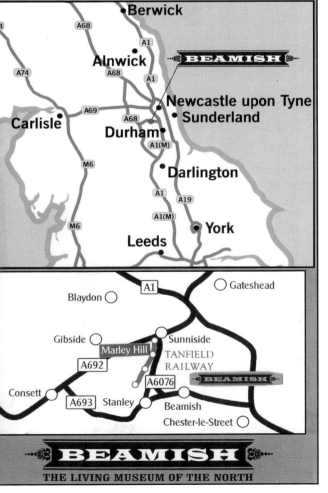

ACKNOWLEDGEMENTS

Paul Jarman has been fortunate to work at Beamish since 2004, and Roger Darsley has followed the development of the Museum since 1966, when the possible dispersion of the 'collection' caused him to write letters to the national and local press. It is easy to become overwhelmed by the breadth and scope of activities at the museum and we are grateful to those photographers who have undertaken to record the transport collection at Beamish in its many guises These individuals are acknowledged in the photographic credits throughout this book, but special mention must be made of J.Harrop and P.Castrey from the Beamish Regional Resource Centre who have not only taken so many of the images, but also suffered our continual pestering throughout the writing of this volume. Our thanks go to L.Brunton, J.Gall, J.Lawson, J.Rees, Christine Stevens and A.Wickens who have contributed information and support to this work and to Norma Darsley for secretarial assistance.

WHAT IS BEAMISH?

At its simplest, Beamish is a museum which preserves something of the past way of life of North East England and presents this to its visitors using the 'open air museum' technique first introduced by Artur Hazeluis in Sweden in the last decade of the nineteenth century.

Beamish is about people, how they worked, played, lived and died. It is about toughness and tenacity, inventiveness and ingenuity, gaiety and tragedy. It is a way of bringing back history so that it can be 'experienced' not just as conservation or as a leisure activity, though it is both, but as a help to understanding the past of the North East and as a spur to its future.

While the North East was the cradle for many developments in engineering and in agriculture, it is perhaps best known for its transport history. It nurtured the waggon ways and saw their development into railways first in the region and then across the country and the world.

Beamish has been around now for forty years. Within its railway history it portrays the wooden waggon way, the coming of steam railways, the link of railways with coal and then with travel in general. This book attempts to show in photographs how this has been planned and developed within the site over those forty years.

THE HISTORY OF THE BEAMISH MUSEUM

In late 1958 a report was made to Durham County Council Museum Committee recommending that collections be built up of the everyday history of the County for an eventual open air museum on a site at Ayckley Heads near Durham City. It so happened that Durham County Council had recently assumed the responsibility for the Bowes Museum near Barnard Castle, a museum largely concerned with continental fine and applied art. Frank Atkinson had just been appointed as Director of the Bowes Museum and realised that the North East region around him was changing dramatically. The old industries of coal-mining, shipbuilding and iron and steel manufacture were disappearing along with the communities that served them. He was most concerned that the identity, customs, traditions and ways of speech should be recorded before they were lost forever.

He proposed that the new museum would illustrate vividly the way of life of the ordinary people and attempt to make the history of the region live. He adopted a policy of unselective collecting and caught the imagination of people in the region. Early collections were stored at Barford Camp, near Barnard Castle, but soon the whole army camp at Brancepeth was full of donations and a bond between the museum and community was formed.

The project was almost ready for implementation in 1966. Durham County Council then considered that this might be of regional importance. They invited all the Local Authorities of the Northern Region to participate. A working party was appointed which operated until 1968 and after many trials and tribulations a Joint Agreement was signed in February 1970 between eight Authorities from the North East. Members of staff were appointed during 1970, with the Director taking up his post in August, and it seems appropriate to treat 1970 as the natal date of Beamish.

A list of possible sites for the museum was considered – Hermitage, Aydon Castle, Corstopitum near Corbridge, Dilston Hall, Bywell, Gibside, Ravensworth, Waldridge Fell, Lambton Castle, Lumley Castle and a little known estate in the Beamish Valley. After extensive negotiations, Beamish Hall and some 300 acres of land were purchased from the National Coal Board. Beamish is a basin-shaped valley with steep slopes, a river, woodland areas, some level ground and a south-facing aspect. Beamish Hall was once the home of the Shafto and Eden families.

The museum has always attracted a large group of influential friends and volunteers. In 1968 they came together formally as The Friends of the Regional Open Air Museum. In 1971, the first exhibition was held in Beamish Hall and in 1972 visitors were able to see the Foulbridge cottages and smithy. Today Beamish is the treasure-house of the region and England's finest open air museum of social, industrial and agricultural heritage. As one of the North's major tourist attractions, Beamish now also makes a major contribution to employment and the regeneration of the region.

The Museum is presently divided into two time zones, 1825 and 1913. The early nineteenth century was a period of great potential but also of social turmoil. Napoleon had been defeated in 1815 but George IV had a restless nation to rule. The North East pioneered agricultural developments particularly in livestock breeding, but it is best known for its industrial development. The increased demand for coal meant a rapid increase in the number of pits away from the banks of the rivers Tyne and Wear. This led to the development of waggon ways and pit communities and eventually to the adoption of railways throughout the world. Pockerley Manor and Farm and the Pockerley Waggon ways are set in this period.

The period between 1900 and 1913 was of particular importance in the history of the North East. Teesside was producing one third of the nation's iron output. The shipyards on the Tyne and Wear were producing two thirds of the national shipping tonnage. In 1913 production from the Great Northern Coalfield was at its peak and by 1914 a substantial proportion of British and World Trade originated in the North East. The Town, Colliery village and Home Farm are set in this period.

The museum is a major educational resource with its regionally significant collections, and its Regional Resource Centre. Opened in 2001, the latter has many collections including photographs, printed books, oral history and objects such as quilts and colliery banners. The Museum has won many awards such as British Museum of the Year and European Museum of the Year. With all of this, the museum functions well, delighting some 400,000 visitors per annum who provide 98% of the annual income required to operate Beamish. Above all, it is still a great day out!

GEOGRAPHICAL SETTING

References to Beamish Valley go back to 1277 in the Shafto papers and Pockerley appears in 1183. (County Durham was not in the Doomsday Book of 1086 which stopped short at the Tees.) In 1786 Beamish was described as a wooded vale on the banks of the River Team which had ten mills or more for the working of iron, making oil, fulling and grinding corn. The fulling mill was later adapted for grinding flints for the Sunderland potteries. The village was then called Pit Hill with the first drift mine opened in 1763 and later a number of deep mines were sunk in the area – Beamish Air Pit (1849), the Chophill (1855) and the Beamish Mary (1883).

There were wooden waggon ways in this area for over 100 years before the coming of railways in 1834. There were three groupings, the first from Tanfield to the Tyne at Dunston with the Causey Arch of 1727. The second group which led to the Tyne east of Newcastle was the Pelaw Main waggon way of 1809 and the Springwell waggon way of 1826. The third group led to the north bank of the River Wear and included the Pelton Fell waggon way of 1693, the Beamish waggon way of 1763, the Waldridge Fell waggon way of 1779 and the Harrington Outside waggon ways of 1787.

The first railway was the Stanhope & Tyne Railway (S&TR) of 1834 which passed to the south of Beamish. Reorganised as the Pontop of South Shields Railway in 1840, it became part of the North Eastern Railway (NER) in 1864. The line was operated with rope worked inclines as well as steam engines and in 1893 the NER built a six and one half mile deviation from Annfield Plain to South Pelaw to allow steam working throughout. This brought the railway into Beamish and Beamish station was opened to goods traffic on 13th November 1893 and to passengers on 1st February 1894.

The NER line tunnelled under the sidings of the Beamish waggon way (which was there first!). The Beamish waggon way was modernised in 1830 and in 1853 was sold with the collieries to the Joicey family becoming the Beamish Railway when steam locomotives were introduced in 1872. The locomotives were serviced at Beamish Engine Works. In 1947 the Beamish Railway became part of the National Coal Board (NCB) and finally closed on 26th March 1966 with the end of mining at the Beamish Mary pit.

The NER became part of the London & North Eastern Railway (LNER) in 1923 and then of British Railways (BR) in 1948. Passenger services were withdrawn from Beamish station in 1953 and from the whole line on 23rd May 1955. Goods services were withdrawn from Beamish station on 2nd August 1960 and from the whole line in 1982 after the Consett Ironworks had closed in October 1980. The track bed of the BR line is now part of Route 7 coast to coast cycle track but the track bed of the Beamish Railway has been largely lost in more recent developments.

GREAT RAILWAY ERA

The genesis of this book came from the realisation that many of the transport items in the Beamish collection had been in the museum's care far longer than they had ever served their original owners and others were now reaching significant milestones in their lives at Beamish. The development of the site from 1970 is worthy of recording, as there have been four decades of collecting, moving, restoring and operating the now extensive collection at the museum. It is incredible to think that, opening in 1973, the Beamish tramway has now been in operation for much longer than many municipal operators in the heyday of street tramways at the turn of the 20th century.

The tramway carries some one million passenger-journeys per annum over a challenging circuit of hills and curves; the waggon way locomotives are in daily steam from Easter until mid-autumn and the reawakening of the railway (left to sleep in the early 1990s) places further pressure on equipment dating back to the early 1870s.

The challenges for any museum with such a large and diverse collection of objects (of which the transport collection is but a part and railed transport a part within this) is to match the public appetite for new developments and displays with the need to conserve and manage an increasingly elderly, fragile and valuable portfolio.

We hope that this selection of views will satisfy the many requests for a narrative on the rail collections at Beamish. There are other excellent works on the historical side of most of the items featured here, so we have deliberately focussed on the life of the collection in museum ownership. Beamish Museum has shown the way for other museums within the country and abroad and has developed a Great Railway Era of its own.

1. INTRODUCTION

In order to follow the development of the Museum's rail heritage we have divided the photographs into four groups; The Railway station, The Tramway, The Colliery Yard and the Waggon Way. Within each the order of photographs is roughly along the time line from 1970 to 2010. The photographs are from the Beamish Resource Centre collection unless otherwise attributed in the captions.

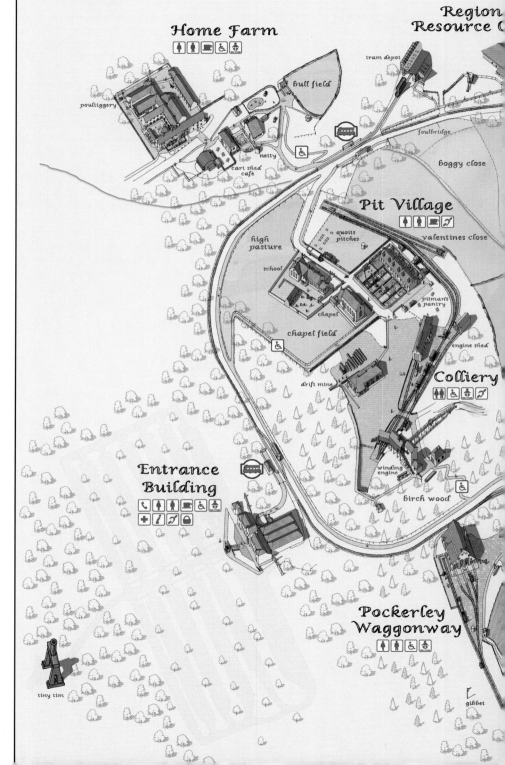

I. The Museum map for 2010

Home Farm

Home Farm

bull field

tram depot

poultiggery

foulbridge

netty

boggy close

cart shed
cafe

Pit Village

high
pasture

quoits
pitches

valentines close

school

pitman's
pantry

chapel

engine shed

chapel field

Colliery

drift mine

Entrance
Building

winding
engine

birch wood

Pockerley
Waggonway

tiny tim

gibbet

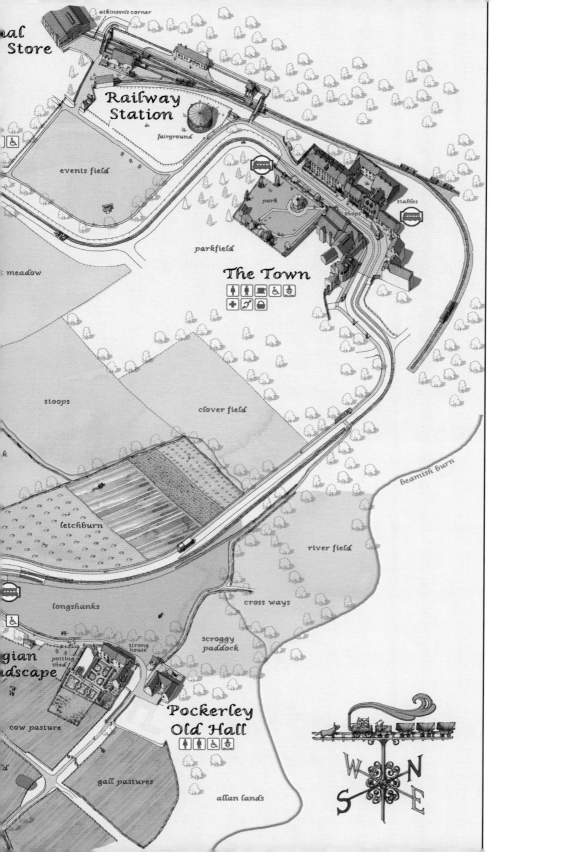

1.1. This aerial view of the Museum in 2009 shows the land form represented by map I. In the foreground are the Town, the railway station and the regional store. To the west are the Regional Resource Centre, the workshops and the tram shed. In the distance is the colliery village with the waggon way running to the east. Beyond the entrance building are the serried ranks of visitors' cars.

1.2. At the entrance building stands a restored chaldron waggon, the symbol of the Museum and of the North East coal trade and its technology. A Newcastle 'chaldron' was 53 cwt (2.6 tonnes). This type of waggon lasted from the 18th century until 1970 when the last were withdrawn from Seaham Harbour. (P.D.Jarman)

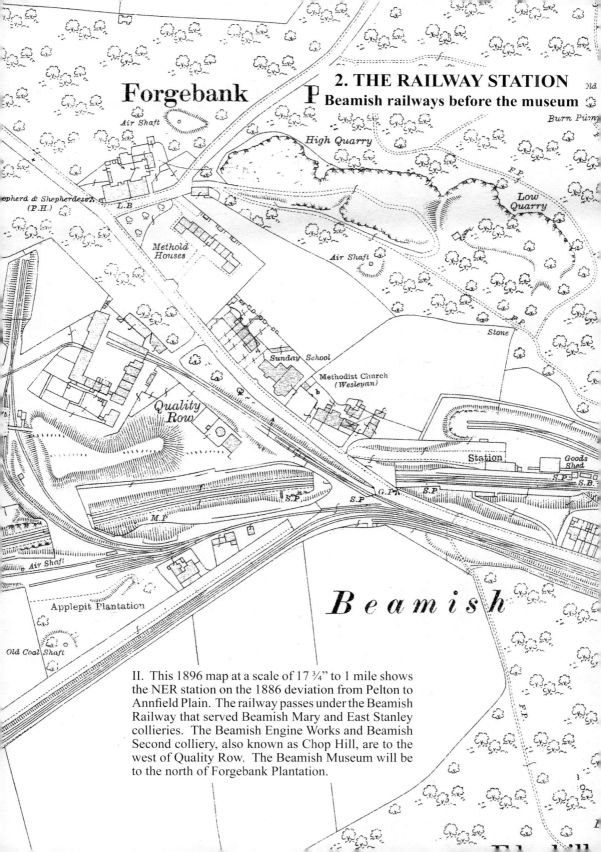

Forgebank

Burn Pump

Air Shaft

High Quarry

Low Quarry

epherd & Shepherdess
(P.H.)

L.B

F.P.

Methold Houses

Air Shaft

Stone

Sunday School

Methodist Church
(Wesleyan)

Quality Row

Station

Goods Shed

S.P.

S.B.

S.P.

M.P.

S.P.

G.P.

S.P.

Air Shaft

Applepit Plantation

Beamish

Old Coal Shaft

II. This 1896 map at a scale of 17 ¾" to 1 mile shows the NER station on the 1886 deviation from Pelton to Annfield Plain. The railway passes under the Beamish Railway that served Beamish Mary and East Stanley collieries. The Beamish Engine Works and Beamish Second colliery, also known as Chop Hill, are to the west of Quality Row. The Beamish Museum will be to the north of Forgebank Plantation.

2.1. The station opened in 1894 and this is an Auty postcard looking west. The piles on the platform are rockery beds. The down line, to Consett, only had a small waiting room. In the background are Quality Row and the faint outline of Beamish Mary colliery. (G. Nairn coll.)

2.2. The wooden station buildings on the up platform are seen more clearly in this view towards Pelton. The goods shed to the left of the signal box was served by a short siding. Three more sidings fanned out across the yard. Parcel traffic to Consett appears to be only one half-barrel! (G.Nairn coll.)

For other views of Beamish station see
*Consett to South Shields
via Beamish*

2.3. British Railways class V3 2-6-2T no.67656 is on a train for Consett and Blackhill. Beamish station closed in 1953, two years before all the passenger services on the line. The buildings other than the signal box have been removed. (Armstrong Railway Photographic Trust)

2.4. Class Q6 0-8-0 no.63444 comes through the short tunnels under the Beamish Railway on 10th June 1961. Freight traffic, mainly coal and iron ore, continued until the closure of Consett Ironworks in October 1980. The railway was abandoned in 1982 and now as Route 7 coast to coast cycle path and walkway is well known for its outdoor artworks such as the metal cows at Beamish. (P.B.Booth/N.E.Stead coll.)

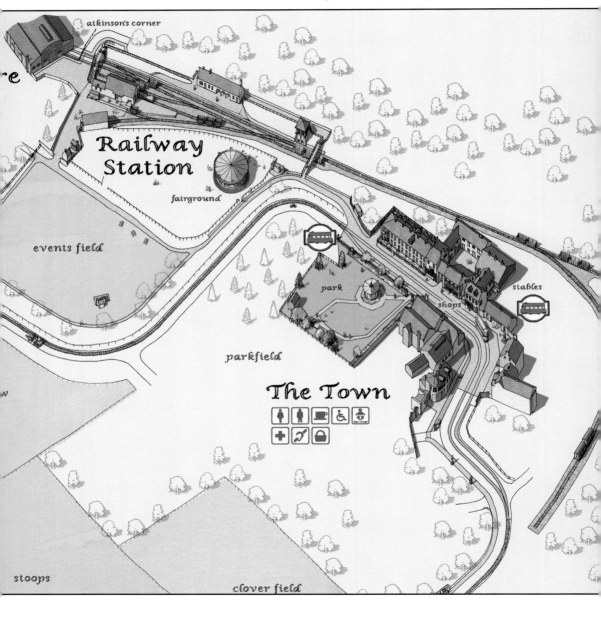

Rowley station in service

2.5. The first station was called Cold Rowley when it opened in 1845. This station was built in 1867 and renamed Rowley in 1868. In a 1904 W.Bainbridge photograph, a NER class 910 2-4-0 locomotive is leaving for Stanhope with a passenger train. The school is prominent and on the hazy horizon are the houses of Consett. (G.Nairn coll.)

2.6. This view towards the moors of a snowbound Rowley station was taken by W.Bainbridge on 29th January 1910. This sort of weather was why the station's original name was Cold Rowley! (G.Nairn coll.)

2.7. The station closed to passengers in 1939, when passenger services between Consett and Stanhope ceased. Occasional excursions were run and there is considerable decay around as an immaculate class K1 2-6-0 no.62027 passes by with the RCTS/SLS 'North Eastern Tour' on 28th September 1962. The line was closed to freight in 1969.

2.8. Rowley is reborn. The roof is nearly tiled, the coping edge wall for the platform is finished, the cutting is cut and a rather forlorn coach is already on site. Rowley is now Beamish station.

2.9. The formal opening of Beamish station was carried out with gusto by Sir John Betjeman on 19th July in 1976. The driver on that day was Albert Johnson of Kibblesworth and the engine was class J21 0-6-0 NER no.876 (65033) and we will see more of it later. (Manchester Guardian/ Beamish coll.)

John Betjeman's Poem on the occasion of opening the station.

TRAIN STRAM AT BEAMISH

Stations are sentimental places where
We say good-bye to those for whom we care;
Conversely, they're the spots where you and I
To those for whom we don't can say good-bye.
Stand on the platform. Feelings, God knows whose,
Come welling up inside you through your shoes,
Feelings of hunger not so very old
In workmans' trains on mornings dark and cold;
Feelings of freedom and unbounded joy
Starting for holidays when you're a boy.
Students tred carefully, the place is holy
It's now in Beamish and once was Rowley.

John Betjeman

Monday July 19 1976

First steps at Beamish

2.10. In the beginning the number of useable vehicles was small and Lambton, Hetton of Joicey Collieries 0-4-0ST no.14 built by Hawthorn Leslie (no.3056 of 1914) hauled the Forcett coach and a NER birdcage brake van no.44824. Passenger numbers look small as well! The Forcett coach was built by the Stockton & Darlington Railway in 1864/5 as no.179 for market day traffic. It was sold in November 1884 to the Forcett Quarry in South Durham. In 1984 it was moved to Shildon then to Hackworth Museum and finally to 'Locomotion'. In 2011 it returned to Beamish.

2.11. The collection of vehicles has grown in this scene of October 1979. In the station yard is 0-6-0T *Twizell* on the passenger train. The J21 0-6-0 and E1 2-4-0CT are in among the goods wagons. Newly re-assembled is the goods shed from Alnwick with fittings from Hexham. Look also at the intricate pointwork in the foreground. (R.R.Darsley)

2.12. *Twizell* an 0-6-0T built by Robert Stephenson in 1891, their no.2730, leaves on a 'mixed' train of the Forcett coach, a 20 ton NER hopper wagon and the NER guards van. The square tank wagon is a water wagon converted from a S&DR tender. Crowds are watching from the town end footbridge which came from Howden le Wear and is a wrought iron sectional pedestrian bridge available from numerous manufacturers.

2.13. An overall view of the station area is given from the footbridge at the goods yard end. Operating signals are controlled from the NER signal box which was originally built around 1897 for Carr House, near Consett. It is fully equipped with the original lever frame and it was refurbished in 2007. (R.R.Darsley)

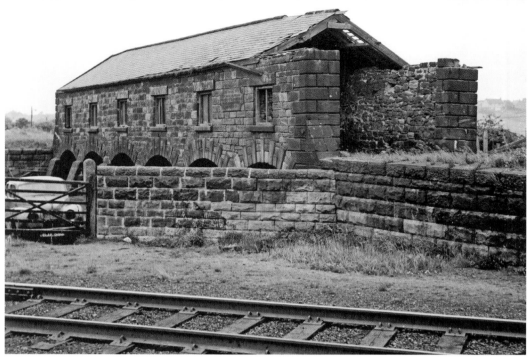

2.14. This is the coal drop and lime depot built at West Boldon on the Stanhope & Tyne Railway in 1865. Unlike most railway companies the NER favoured hopper discharge unloading mineral wagons. The coal and the corrosive lime were stored under the arches and distributed by local coal and agricultural merchants. (F.Atkinson/Beamish coll.)

2.15. The coal drops are now reinstated in the Beamish goods yard. Inside is a 10½ ton coal wagon, NER no.1077, built in 1887 to the Diagram P4 which replaced the chaldron waggon. A horse-drawn coal dray is in one of the arches. (R.R.Darsley)

2.16. Here we can see the NER ground mounted footbridge of the 1860 period from Dunston, and the Alnwick goods shed with a substantial goods office attached that provides staff facilities. The open end of the coal drops is in front of the goods shed. On the right are the wooden coal office from Hexham and the stone built weigh cabin from Glanton on the Alnwick to Wooler line.

2.17. This is the storage area behind the Town, with all sorts of materials as well as Class J21 0-6-0 and 0-4-0ST no.5 *Malleable*, coaches, and vans. The 10-ton inflammable liquid tank wagon, no.125, ended up in Consett Iron Works. The flat wagon, with a tarred shed (the bait room) on it, is from South Shields pier railway. It is the last NER fire engine wagon, no.03938, built in 1901, which carried a steam fire engine and was placed at strategic points around the timber stores at Tyne Dock. (R.R.Darsley)

2.18.   Other storage space and a workshop for early restoration was provided at Marley Hill, the 1854 engine shed of the Bowes Railway and now the headquarters of the Tanfield Railway. This 1970 photograph shows the interior of the shed with three NCB locomotives at the far end. (F.Atkinson/Beamish coll.)

2.19.   *Twizell* came to Beamish on 17th March 1972 and initially was stored at Marley Hill, where it is seen partially dismantled and in the company of Consett A no.5 0-6-0PT (Kitson 2509 of 1883) now at the Stephenson Museum, North Shields, and NCB no.38 0-6-0T Hudswell Clarke 1823 of 1947.   After some use on the Beamish railway trains, Twizell was employed as a stationary boiler supplying steam to the 1855 colliery winder from Chophill Pit.

2.20. The NCB Ashington railway system ran workmen's trains which used NER elliptical roofed carriages. When these trains ceased in 1967, no.9300/164, built in 1911, and no.9300/163 (NER 118), built in 1913, were acquired by Beamish and taken to Templetown works, Consett, for storage.

2.21. They were then brought down to the sidings area at Beamish in 1973, where the end of one is seen in the company of the NER snowplough, no.20 of 1909 from Darlington, and three NER clerestory coaches, nos. 3071, s818 and 1172, also from the Ashington system.

2.22. The coaches are obviously a long term project but one of the difficulties is finding somewhere sheltered from the elements to do the restoration. One idea was to build a poly-tunnel over one of the sidings and here its construction is beginning.

2.23. One coach was restored to its original condition in 1981 and used on the passenger train. It carries the number 818 but is actually 3071. However, standing outside in all weathers began to undo the good work. An agreement with the Tanfield Railway has seen nos.3071 (818), s818 (the real one) and 118 moved to Marley Hill for long term restoration with Tanfield, though 3071 will return home to Beamish in 2011.

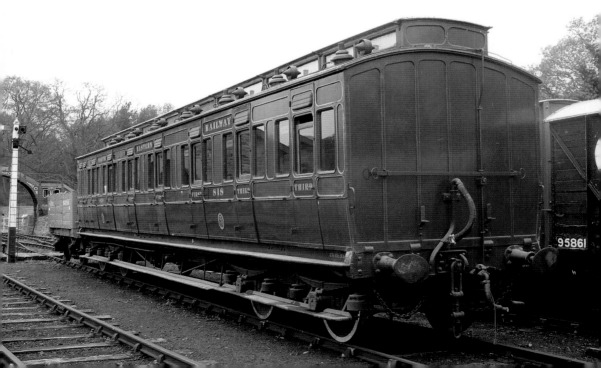

The Big Engine

2.24. NER class C 0-6-0 no.876, was built in 1889 as a Von Borries compound locomotive with Joy valve gear. It was later rebuilt as a 'simple' (without the compounding system that used the steam twice) and with Stephenson Link valve gear. It became J21 no.5033 in LNER days and 65033 with the BR. It was shedded at Hexham and on 11th January 1955 it was fitted with a small snow plough. (R.R.Darsley)

2.25. In 1939 no.5033 was withdrawn from service but the advent of World War II saw it reinstated to work for another 24 years. It was used for passenger and freight trains and, towards the end of its BR life, it was a favourite for local rail tours. This is a RCTS excursion from Darlington to Carlisle via Tebay at Barnard Castle station on 7th May 1960. (A.J.Wickens)

2.26. No.65033 was turned down for preservation by the National Railway Museum (NRM) because of its rebuilding from compound to simple. It had already been sold to a scrap merchant but Frank Atkinson managed to save it and move it to the Templetown shed of the British Steel's Consett works.

2.27. In 1975 it was moved to Marley Hill where it was restored by apprentices from Clark Chapman. A Smith Rodley vertical boilered steam crane, now also at Beamish, is lifting the top of the cab to allow better access to the fire box. It was painted in NER livery and renumbered 876.

2.28. These two locomotives 0-4-0ST LHJC no.14 and 0-6-0 NER no.876 were the stalwarts of the early days of the passenger service. No.876 is in full lined out livery. No.14 sports a flower wreath which is a Beamish tradition for special days.

2.29. On the 25th June 2003, class J21 no.65033 was repainted in the BR livery and J15 0-6-0 no.65463 arrived from the North Norfolk Railway to keep it company, before it departed for the Flour Mill engine works. Both locomotives were designed by T.W.Worsdell. (R.R.Darsley)

2.30. On its way, no.65033 visited the Doncaster Works Open Day on 27th July 2003. After some time at the North Norfolk Railway, the locomotive became the property of the Locomotive Conservation and Learning Trust and moved to Shildon. A joint conservation project with the NRM will see its restoration together with bogie stores van no.5523. No.65033 will be 125 years old in 2014 which is the target date for completion. (K.Swann/Beamish coll.)

2.31. In 1980, the country celebrated the 150th anniversary of the Liverpool and Manchester Railway and the Rainhill trials. Replicas of the original locomotives were made and the trials run again. In the foreground at Beamish is the replica *Rocket*; behind is the replica *Sans Pareil* and the BBC television crew.

2.32. The camera crew has a railway track of its own, as they film *Sans Pareil*. *Novelty* was the only other contestant in the original trials and in the re-run. Despite the enthusiasm of the fans of Hackworth's *Sans Pareil*, the result of the re-run was the same as the original. Stephenson's *Rocket* was the winner and the design for the future development of locomotives.

'Rowley' awakes

2.33. After slumbering from the mid 1980s, the railway station awoke and from 2006 demonstration trains were worked at weekends with visiting steam locomotives. Posed between the gas light and the Beamish Waggon and Iron Works (The Regional Store built in 2000) is 0-4-0ST *W.S.T,* built by Andrew Barclay no.2361 of 1954. The loco was visiting from the Bowes Railway at Springwell in April 2006. (P.D.Jarman)

2.34. Another visitor that year from the Bowes Railway was NCB no.22 (85) also a 0-4-0ST built by Andrew Barclay, no.2274 of 1949. The shovel on the coal heap is a North East coal miner's shovel with its 'spade' shape. (P.D.Jarman)

2.35. Passenger services began again in 2010. The first train on 1st April was formed of *Renishaw Ironworks no.6* 0-6-0ST Hudswell Clarke no.1366 of 1919 from Tanfield and the NER saloon from the Furness Railway Trust. No.6 visited in April and May and is seen ready to leave the station. (P.D.Jarman)

2.36. 0-6-0WT *Bellerophon* visited in September 2010. It is owned by the Vintage Carriage Trust and currently lodges at the Foxfield Railway in Staffordshire. The locomotive was designed by Josiah Evans of Haydock Foundry for collieries in the St Helen's area. The two 4-wheel coaches were loaned from the Tanfield Railway. These were TR no.7 (ex-NER officers' coach no.853) and TR no.9 (ex-NER 3rd class 256). (P.D.Jarman)

2.37. At the end of the line is 0-4-0ST *Sir Cecil A. Cochrane*, built locally by Robert Stephenson & Hawthorns of Newcastle, no.7409, in 1948. It worked at Dunston and is a regular performer at the Tanfield Railway. It visited Beamish in August and September 2010. (P.D.Jarman)

2.38. Furness Railway 0-4-0 no.20 is the oldest working locomotive, built by Sharp & Stewart & Co. in 1863, restored in 1998 to its original condition, having been converted to an 0-4-0ST while in colliery service in Manchester. It was the visiting locomotive in September 2008 and in June and July 2010. The coach is Great Eastern Railway no.5 formerly the royal saloon of Princess Alexandra and used as an engineers' coach until 1972. It is owned by the Furness Railway Trust. (D.Hewitt)

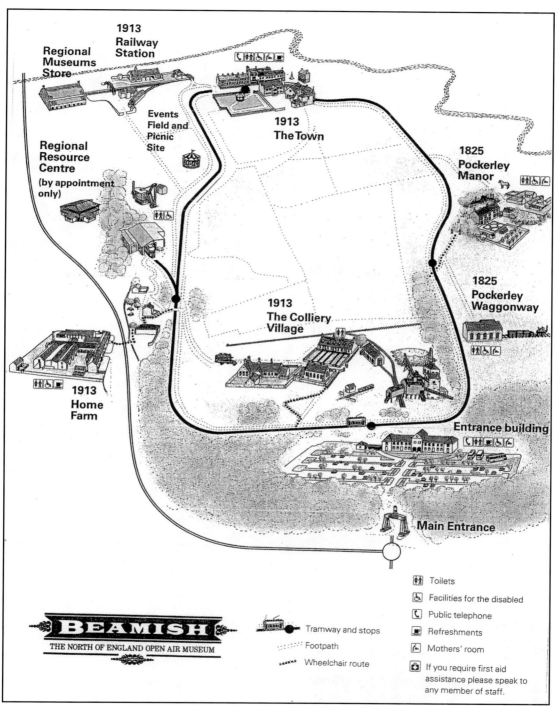

1913
Railway
Station

Regional
Museums
Store

Events
Field and
Picnic
Site

1913
The Town

1825
Pockerley
Manor

Regional
Resource
Centre
(by appointment
only)

1825
Pockerley
Waggonway

1913
The Colliery
Village

1913
Home
Farm

Entrance building

Main Entrance

BEAMISH
THE NORTH OF ENGLAND OPEN AIR MUSEUM

Tramway and stops
Footpath
Wheelchair route

Toilets
Facilities for the disabled
Public telephone
Refreshments
Mothers' room
If you require first aid
assistance please speak to
any member of staff.

IV. The older Beamish Museum map shows the tramway circuit in clear outline.

3. THE TRAMWAY

Early days at Consett

3.1. Before the opening of the Beamish tramway, a lot of hard work was done by the Northern Tramway Sponsors at the Consett Iron Company premises at Templetown. Here the Tramway group are working on Sheffield Corporation Tramways no.342. It survived in service until 1956 and then went to the British Transport Commission transport museum at Clapham. In 1967 it was removed to Consett.
(G.Hearse/
Beamish coll.)

3.2. Tram no.342 was originally no.264. At Consett it was temporarily converted to an open top layout because of the poor condition of the upper deck structure. It was painted in Gateshead colours, renumbered no.1 and transferred to Beamish in December 1973. It is being trialled at Consett on a short test run in the company of Gateshead no.10.
(G.Hearse/
Beamish coll.)

The electric tramway is built

3.3. The surveyors are out at Beamish, as the first peg is hammered in to start the construction of Beamish tramway in January 1973. One of the early ideas was that the tramway would run from the visitor centre to the town on the west side and the railway from the station to the colliery village on the east side.

3.4. Track laying was a very manual affair in January 1973. Trams run on railway track in the country areas but grooved tram-track, visible in the foreground is used in the streets and tarmacadam areas. Trams can climb steeper inclines than railways and down the hill is Gateshead no.10. The steepest gradient is Pockerley bank at 1 in 16.

3.5. The electric supply to the trams is supplied by overhead cables with the trams having poles with pulley connectors. The overhead wiring is fitted and maintained from extension towers. Here in 1973 Frank Hewitson is assisting Peter Price to assemble overhead tramway wires using a Thorneycroft tower wagon from the County Borough of Stockport. The first section of tramway was formally inspected for use on 25th May 1973.

3.6. The first trams used on the tramway were Gateshead no.10 and no.1 (no.342). The Gateshead and District Tramways Co. built no.10 in their Sunderland Road works in 1926. When the Gateshead system closed in 1951, it and 18 other similar trams went to the British Railways electric railway between Grimsby and Immingham, where it was no.26. This closed on 1st July 1961 but the British Transport Commission put it aside for preservation. (G.Hearse/Beamish coll..)

Some tramcar histories

3.7.   Gateshead no.10 is 42ft 8ins long with longitudinal seating for 48 passengers. The tram worked routes in Gateshead and across the River Tyne to Newcastle and Gosforth and has the distinctive arrangement of front exit and rear entrance, denoted by the large triangular notice on the dash panels. One of the sister trams, Gateshead no.5, can be seen at the National Tramway Museum at Crich, Derbyshire.

3.8. In 1968 the Northern Tramway Sponsors arranged for no.10 to go to Consett Iron Company where it was restored to its original guise. Its equipment is a pair of Brill 39E reversed maximum traction bogies with Dick Kerr DK31A 35 hp motors operated from English Electric DB1 K3 controllers. (G.Hearse/Beamish coll.)

3.9. In 1973 no.10 arrived at the Foulbridge stop with passengers disembarking from the rear despite the notices. By 2010, the fashions had changed and the tramway now carries one million passenger-journeys a year.

3.10. At the Town terminus no.10 pauses before setting off again. Note the beautiful street lights with the overhead arms. No.10 is the most iconic tram on the system and one author (RRD) can remember, as a boy, travelling from Gosforth to Gateshead on the 'Low Fell square wheelers'. (R.R.Darsley)

3.11. One of the problems for museum staff is that these veteran trams are today working as hard as they did in their original life. No.10 received a major rebuild between 1983 and 1985 and now appears in late 1920s condition. 0-4-0ST *W.S.T.* is on a demonstration freight in 2007. (P.D.Jarman)

3.12. The Glasgow underground railway was modernised in 1978 and six of the old underground coaches were brought to Beamish. They were not for restoration, as the gauge and traction pick up were not compatible, but were for the electrical parts and vintage fittings which are hard to find. This was 22nd October 1979. Some life-expired frames still remained in 2010. (R.R.Darsley)

3.13. Blackpool has a history of continuous tramway operation which in 2010 is being modernised. Blackpool Corporation no.31 was built in 1901 by the Midland Railway Carriage & Wagon Co. It was transferred to the Engineering Department in 1934 as no.4 and in 1960 renumbered 754. On 25th May 1980 it is hiding behind its sister tram, no.753, in the back of the car sheds at Blackpool. No.754 was painted plain green and no.753 was green and white. (R.R.Darsley)

3.14. In 1920 Blackpool rebuilt no.31 as a bogie car before producing its 'standard' cars. The rebuilt body was on a pair of English Electric 4ft wheelbase equal-wheel bogies each with a BTH 265C 35hp motor and the tram is equipped with BTH 510 controllers. In July 1984 it was transferred on long-term loan to Beamish for restoration. This took four years in the Beamish workshops. When it emerged, it was as no.31.

3.15. This very popular tram now operates regularly every summer as an open top double deck Blackpool tram no.31 in its 1920s condition. Here it is at Pockerley with Gateshead no.10 on 4th August 2006. (R.R.Darsley)

3.16. As Engineering car no.4, no.31 survived for 50 years and for the 'Power from the Past' weekend on 15th-18th April 2010 it was repainted in green and white and numbered 4. Beamish also has Blackpool Tower wagon no.749 in store.

← 3.17. Blackpool has heritage days when preserved trams from Blackpool's fleet and other fleets run on the Blackpool sea front. Here is Beamish's no.31 passing the famous Tower on 29th September 2010. In November 2010 it was on loan to Heaton Park Tramway, Manchester. (P.D.Jarman)

← 3.18. Blackpool may be famous for its illuminated trams but Beamish can also put on a show as no.31 demonstrates here. Running trams at night with lights ablaze is a highly popular activity at the museum.

3.19. In the Sheffield Corporation car sheds were those trams in the final procession when the system closed in 1960. No.513, the tram on the left, came to Beamish, while the other four went to the National Tramway Museum. Nos.513 and 510 were built between 1950 and 1952 by Charles Roberts & Co. to a Sheffield Transport design. They represented the ultimate development of the traditional British four-wheel tramcar.

3.20. No.513 was purchased by Mr. J Rothera of York. After 16 years of storage it arrived at Beamish in 1976. Restoration commenced in 1978. The tram has a four-wheel Maley and Taunton hornless type 588 truck, powered by two Metrovick 101 DR3 65hp motors and fitted with a pair of Crompton-West CT/TJ controllers. It entered service at Beamish in 1983 in standard Sheffield livery.

3.21. On 24th October 1984, no.513 left for Blackpool, where it operated on loan for 14 months taking part in the Blackpool Tramway Centenary celebrations on September 1985. It returned on 27th December 1985. No.513 went again on long-term loan to Blackpool departing 15th February 2001. On a low loader it is about to leave the Beamish tram shed. It is a useful all-weather tram but well outside Beamish's historical period.

3.22. Sheffield no.342 was no.1 when it left Consett to work at Beamish. On 5th May 1984 it was still in a Gateshead style livery outside the tram shed, but in 1985 it was decided to restore it to its original 1920s condition as open balcony car no.264. In the picture is the giant steam hammer that is now over the entrance gate to the museum grounds. (R.R.Darsley)

3.23. The rebuilding of no.264 took until 1987, when it emerged in the ornate Sheffield livery of Prussian blue and cream. It had a substantially new top deck incorporating many of the original parts and has been a most useful all weather tram. (D.Foster)

3.24. No.264 was withdrawn from service at the end of the 2003 season needing major restoration to the lower body and some mechanical attention and this will be done when funding becomes available. Here it is at the Foulbridge stop with the colliery village in the valley. (R.R.Darsley)

3.25. Sheffield Corporation no.264 is photographed in all its night time glory. There is a link with the next tram, Newcastle Corporation Tramways 'A' class tramcar no.114, as it and most of the 'A' class were sold to Sheffield in 1940 to replace war damaged vehicles. (P.D.Jarman)

3.26. Newcastle 'A' class tramcar, no.114, was built in 1901 by Hurst Nelson & Co., Motherwell. During their life, this class was extensively rebuilt, one of the early improvements being the addition of a top deck cover. In this form it is seen with tram no.36 working in Gosforth. (A.Williamson coll.)

3.27. No.114 was finally withdrawn in 1952. Its body was discovered on a farm near Scunthorpe, where it had been used as a chicken shed and here it is being recovered. After several moves it arrived at Beamish in 1987. Total rebuilding has been carried out using a mixture of contract, museum and volunteer labour, incorporating as many original parts as was practicable.

3.28. The whole restoration took nine years to complete. A suitable 4-wheel Brill truck with GE 270 motors was acquired from Oporto, Portugal in 1989 and modified to fit no.114 dimensions. Two BTH B18 controllers were installed and the tram totally rewired to modern safety standards. Here it is in the Foulbridge tram shed with Gateshead no.10 and Sunderland no.16. This depot is part of a large workshop complex on the site of Foulbridge farm. (P.D.Jarman)

The trams' full circle

3.29. The tramway had proved to be an efficient mover of people and it was decided to make a full circle of track. Planned in 1992, it was formally opened in 1993. To cope with increasing visitor numbers no.114 was launched into service in May 1996. Here it is departing from the visitor centre tram stop on 11th May 2002. It is now the only example of this type of tram to survive. (R.R.Darsley)

3.30. No.114 was built with wooden seats for 53 passengers and is here seen filled to capacity on 8th July 2006 at the Town stop by Barclay's Bank. The conductor is explaining to a tourist that 'another tram will be along in a minute!' This tram celebrated its 100th birthday on 20th October 2001. (R.R.Darsley)

3.31. This is a posed photograph by the Beamish livery stables. It is hoped that the gentleman on the Sun Inn delivery tricycle will not be arrested for speeding, as he overtakes the tram. As a design, no.114 gave no protection at all to the driver who is totally exposed to all that the weather would throw at him. (P.D.Jarman)

3.32. Oporto tram no.196 was built at the Boavista Works in 1935 by Companhia Carris de Ferro de Porto (The Oporto Tramways Company) as a 28 seater single deck car with a Brill 21E two GE (USA) 270A 55hp motors and B54E controllers. There were 77 similar cars and most survived until Oporto's trams were modernised around 2000. Several came to Britain and to America for preservation projects. This is tram no.203 at Infante, Oporto, on 9th September 2004. (R.R.Darsley)

3.33. Oporto withdrew no.196 after collision damage and it came to Beamish in 1989, to yield spare parts. However, it was in sound condition on arrival so it was decided to make it a totally enclosed car for off-season operation and use tram no.176, for spares. Many parts of the original styling, including notices in Portuguese, were kept. No.196 entered service in 1992. Following body repairs in 2001, it re-entered service with a Gateshead style livery and the fictitious 'Beamish Tramways'. (P.D.Jarman)

The mature tramway

3.34. Not only trams but tramlines need repair and the streets need renewing and such scenes as this were common. Here square sets are being re-laid between the tram lines outside Barclay's Bank and the Masonic Lodge in the Town in October 2005. The mile and a half of heavily used tramway requires continued inspection and repair. (P.D.Jarman)

3.35. Maintenance vehicles used by tramways are seen in this photograph. They are Wallis & Steevens Advance steam roller HO 6496 and Cardiff City works tram no.131. This was built as a water carrier for cleaning and rail grinding work. By oversight, it was left off the list when all the Cardiff trams were scrapped. It was the first tram at the National Tramway Museum at Crich in 1959 and was restored for Crich's 50th anniversary in 2009. It made a brief appearance at Beamish 15th-18th April, 2010. (P.D.Jarman)

3.36. Another road roller, and another engineering tram, are in the Town centre. PY 6070 is a Fowler road roller. No.6 was built by Hurst Nelson for Hull Corporation as no.96 in 1901. It was an open topped double-decker which was totally enclosed in 1930 and then cut down to a stores vehicle and snow plough in 1933. Sold to Leeds 1942-5, it was their stores vehicle no.6 until 1959. It went to Heaton Park Tramway in 1988 and came on loan to Beamish from 15th April, 2010. (J.Cross/Beamish coll.)

3.37. Sunderland Corporation Tramways made a valiant effort after World War II to modernise their system. No.16 is wearing the striking red and white livery and the famous 'Shop at Binns' advert. (S.Lockwood coll.)

3.38. When the Sunderland Corporation Tramways closed in 1954, a number of tram bodies escaped burning. After a spell as changing-rooms on a football field, the lower saloon of no.16 became a tool-shed and apple store at Westwood Farm, Low Warden, near Hexham, Northumberland. It was moved to Beamish in 1989 for a restoration. (J.Gall/Beamish coll.)

3.39. The tram was built as an open-top tramcar by Dick Kerr & Co, Preston, in 1900 in a batch of six trams, nos.13-18. The class received its top cover after the Great War. Further modifications followed in the 1920s and 1930s. Fifty years after it was withdrawn in Sunderland, no.16 was relaunched into service at Beamish on 2nd July, 2003 by Kate Adie, who came from that city. No.16 is at the Beamish tram shed with nos.114 and 196. (P.D.Jarman)

3.40. No16 was restored to its 1920s enclosed double deck condition to represent the second largest tramway undertaking in the North East with monies from the European Regional Development Fund. It has been fitted with a Peckham P35 truck with 2 BTH 509 electric motors and Dicken/English Electric controllers. While some work was done by specialist commercial firms, a lot of the detailed work was done by Beamish Tramway Group. It is passing the back of the Visitor Centre en route for Pockerley. (R.R.Darsley)

3.41. The mature tramway is now a place for visitors such as the precursor of the electric tram, the horse tram. L53 is the sole survivor of Manchester's horse tram fleet. It was built in 1880 with Eades patent reversible body which rotated on the frame thus needing only one staircase. It was discovered in 1970, still on its wheels, as a holiday home at Glossop, Derbyshire. At Heaton Park from 1998 it was in operation from 2008 and has been based at Bury Transport Museum since May 2010. (P.D.Jarman)

3.42. Observant visitors will notice the twin wires of trolley bus overhead wiring in the Foulbridge area. From 1935 Newcastle Corporation Transport introduced trolleybuses to replace trams. No.501 is the only survivor of 30 Sunbeam S7 three axle trolleybuses and was delivered on 27th July 1948. Withdrawn on 30th May 1965, no.501 arrived at Beamish in 1974. Restoration was done by the Beamish Tramway Group. Too modern for Beamish, it travels away frequently. Here it is at Sandtoft Transport Centre near Doncaster beside a Bradford two axle trolleybus. (P.D.Jarman)

3.43. The period of the Town and Village is 1913 and there were trolleybuses shortly after that time. Not only that but Beamish has one that belonged to Keighley Corporation. This photograph shows no.12 (registered WT 7108) on arrival in the West Yorkshire town, one of four bought in 1924 to replace their trams. In 1931 the trolleybuses were abandoned when West Yorkshire took over service provision.
(S.Lockwood coll.)

3.44. No.12 is a Brush built 32 seat body on a Straker-Clough chassis with BTH electrical equipment and a BTH 247 40hp motor. The current collection was from an Estler co-axial trolley base with the poles mounted vertically one above the other. It went to Grassington, near Skipton, where it became a holiday home. In July 1988 it was acquired by Beamish. The original structure is reasonably sound. When resources are available, it will be restored to running order, though not with the original equipment. (P.D.Jarman)

4. THE COLLIERY YARD

V The 6″ to 1 mile map of 1912 shows collieries in the area of Beamish.

Beamish collieries before the museum

4.1. Beamish Mary colliery was to the south west of the village and originally called Beamish Air pit. The Air pit was sunk in 1849 and the Mary shaft 100yards east in 1883. The Air shaft and screens are on the left of this 1912 photograph. In 1952 the colliery was modernised, the scheme being completed in 1956. The colliery closed on 26th March 1966. (G.Nairn coll.)

4.2. *Twizell* is standing in the modernised Beamish Mary colliery yard with the screens and loading gantries behind. Pictures of the actual collieries are rare, most enthusiasts having concentrated on photographing the locomotives. (Armstrong Railway Photographic Trust)

4.3. Beamish Second pit was known as Chop Hill when it was sunk in about 1763. (The First pit is behind the Shepherd and Shepherdess public house and there were also 3rd, 4th, 5th and 6th pits.) Beamish Second colliery had two shafts from 1832 and two drifts from 1931, one of which is the Mahogany Drift in Beamish Museum. The colliery closed in 1962 after 200 years of mining. This is the winding house and headstock in about 1966 after most of the site had been cleared. (G.Nairn coll.)

4.4. 0-6-0T *Twizell* is on its way with a train of 21 ton hopper wagons to Beamish Mary pit along the Beamish Railway. It is approaching the junction for Beamish Engine Works. The railway was operated by rope inclines and horses until 1872. (C.E.Mountford coll.)

4.5. Photographed in 1950, the engine shed at Beamish Engine Works was a single road building. On the left is the lifting gantry and much of the repair work on the locomotive would be done in the open. The museum's Colliery Yard engine shed is based on the same design but is wider to allow visitors safe access. Some of the materials came from this 1870s building. (C.E.Mountford coll.)

4.6. Inside the Beamish Engine Works yard is 0-6-0ST, *Stanley,* Robert Stephenson no.2014 of 1872. It was being 'rebuilt' but it took many years and was never finished. It was scrapped in December 1961. Behind the locomotive is the engine shed and part of the locomotive hoist. A man powered narrow gauge railway is used for moving components around. In the foreground the pulley wheels could be for a rope incline railway. (Armstrong Railway Photographic Trust)

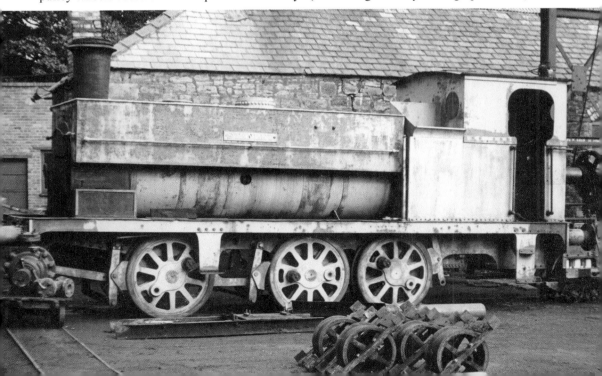

4.7. This is Station Road, Beamish, with the tracks of the Beamish Railway on the left. The station and the NER lines are in a cutting behind the houses. This postcard shows Beamish village as it was in the period reproduced by the Town in Beamish Museum. (G.Nairn.coll.)

4.8. This very early disc signal guarded the level crossing on the Beamish Railway between Chop Hill and West Pelton. When the crossing gates were closed, the disc and light faced the train as here. When they were open, the disc rotated through 90º. The date is 28th March 1966 and on closure of the railway, the signal went to Beamish Museum where it is the starter signal for the Pockerley waggon way. (D.A.Charlton)

Colliery Yard developments

VI The Colliery Yard in 2010.

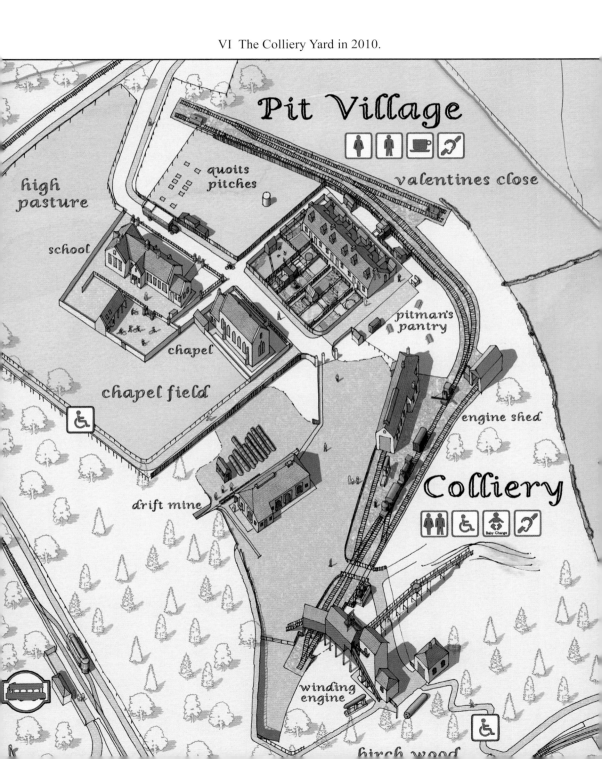

4.9. The museum began to recover industrial artefacts, not only from the Beamish Railway on its doorstep but from farther a-field and this was often challenging. Here the struggle is the collection of a former River Wear Commission side-tipping wagon of the Manchester Ship Canal type that had initially been preserved at the Pallion Museum in Sunderland.

4.10. The early days of the Colliery Yard involved collecting material before it disappeared as scrap. Here on the early sidings laid on coal ash are a large number of chaldron waggons in various states of disrepair, a colliery ventilation shaft fan and a rust covered steam locomotive. Outside its temporary tin shed is the museum work horse, Ruston Hornsby 88DS diesel locomotive, no.47614 of 1963, from the Northern Gas Board.

4.11. It is still early days in the Colliery Yard, as in the background the Chop Hill colliery loading shed is being reassembled. On 22nd October 1979 0-4-0ST no.14 and 0-4-0ST no.5 *Malleable* are slumbering amongst the collected artefacts. *Malleable* came from South Durham Malleable Iron Company Stockton Ironworks. It was withdrawn in 1966 and came to Beamish in 1971. It was steamed at Marley Hill occasionally but since the mid 1970s has been out of use. (R.R.Darsley)

4.12. *Malleable* looks very forlorn in the torrential rain, as it is viewed through the colliery level crossing gate. It is claimed to be built in 1900 by the Stockton Ironworks, but may have origins in a 1870s locomotive from Grange Ironworks of Durham. It was rebuilt by Hunslet of Leeds around 1910, and may also include Black Hawthorn components. Rebuilt again in 1928, it was later re-boiler in 1952 by Robert, Stephenson and Hawthorns so it really is a hybrid locomotive! How would you restore it? (P.D.Jarman)

4.13. This overview of the colliery-yard was taken on 8th May 2001. On the left, the Beamish Engine Shed is complete. The tin shed was originally built to keep the *Locomotion* replica out of the weather. *Malleable* and 'Jacob' the McEwan Pratt patent locomotive, stand in the sidings. On the right are a grounded van body, a restored chaldron waggon, and the pit loading shed. (R.R.Darsley)

4.14. A line of chaldron waggons wait to be filled at Chop Hill. In the stone winding house is the 1855 stationary steam engine, built by J&G Joicey & Co. of Newcastle. Next is the headstock and the screening shed from Ravensworth Park colliery, Gateshead. From the screening shed an elevated narrow gauge railway takes the stones screened out to the waste tip. (R.R.Darsley)

Head Wrightson locomotives

4.15.　　　Head Wrightson & Co. of Thornaby, Teesside, built some distinctive locomotives with vertical boilers known as 'coffee pots'. No.1 was supplied in 1871 to Dorking Greystone Lime Company and worked at their Betchworth Quarry, where it was photographed between 1871 and 1873.

4.16. Redundant in the early 1950s, it was sold back to Head Wrightson in 1960 and restored for display in their works. Here it is with chaldron waggon no.974 at Marley Hill in the 1970s, having arrived there in September 1971.

4.17. No.1 moved to Consett Ironworks in July 1970 and via Marley Hill to Beamish arriving in March 1975. It was given a light overhaul so that it could work on the colliery railway. In 1984 it was restored by ICI, Wilton, and was given a cab which afforded a little shelter to the crew. It ran for a couple of years but was then laid up needing a completely new boiler. (K.Swann/Beamish coll.)

4.18. From late 2006, £100,000 was donated, largely from the Heritage Lottery Fund to enable the complete restoration of no.1 to its 1871 condition. Here, in the colliery engine shed, the frames have been jacked up and the wheels dropped out. No.17, the other Head Wrightson vertical boiler locomotive, has also been dismantled. (P.D.Jarman)

4.19. The new boiler with crankshaft and cylinders is laid out on the floor of Israel Newton's Engine Foundry at Bradford on 23rd April 2009, prior to reassembly. A conventional boiler is in the background. The opportunity was taken to make as many parts as possible that would also be of use in a full restoration of No.17, which has currently only been cosmetically restored. (P.D.Jarman)

4.20. Resplendent in new maroon paint and polished brass work, no.1 stands in the Colliery Yard with a short train of chaldron waggons. The date is 17th April 2010. (P.D.Jarman)

Chaldron waggons and Seaham Harbour

4.21. The chaldron waggon goes back to the standard measure horse-drawn coal waggon which contained one 'chalder' (53cwt) of coal and had a bottom discharge door. Later waggons from the 1860s had the capacity increased to four tons and were locally known as Black waggons because of the black bitumen paint that was the uniform livery. Beamish eventually collected 34 complete or part complete Black waggons in the early 1970s.

4.22. A Black waggon is stripped down to its ironwork for its restoration in 2010. It was common colliery practice to buy wheels, metalwork and castings from local foundries and build their own waggons. This type of waggon can also be seen at the Tanfield Railway, the Bowes Railway, Springwell, and the National Railway Museum at both York and Shildon. (P.D.Jarman)

4.23. No.1 is hauling two chaldron waggons along the colliery line on 17th April 2010. These are L328 and newly restored L1219. The 'L' stands for Londonderry (and not Lambton, as often thought). The Londonderry family owned Seaham Harbour from 1845 to 1899, had an interest in it until 1920 and retained ownership of local collieries until nationalisation in 1947. (P.D.Jarman)

4.24. No.17, Head Wrightson's no.33 was supplied to the Londonderry Railway in 1873. In 1899 it was transferred to the Seaham Harbour Dock Company and worked on the harbour quayside as seen here. Withdrawn in 1962, it was bought by Head Wrightson and, like no.1, displayed at their works. In 1975 it went via the Stockton & Darlington 150th anniversary celebrations to the Darlington Railway Museum. In 2003 it moved to Beamish and was cosmetically restored to its 1950s condition. (D.Young/ Beamish coll.)

4.25. On 9th December 2007, no.17 was returned to Seaham Harbour to mark the 40th anniversary of a major storm and smash at the harbour. The mainly wooden staiths had been removed from the quays by then and the locomotive is on the track just above the boat. The weather was also celebrating the storm, as the waves pour over the outer harbour walls. (J.Harrop/Beamish coll.)

4.26. This is a closer view of the locomotive on the quay, while the waves curl in the background. Whereas no.1 has vertical cylinders driving the wheels through gears, no.17 has inclined outside cylinders which are visible under the stepped running board. (P.D.Jarman)

4.27. The other locomotive that worked the staiths with no.17 was 0-4-0ST, no.18. This view shows the towering staiths that went out onto the quays. The coal wagons went out on top of the staiths and dropped the coal by bottom discharge into chutes and then into the ships. No.18 worked with chaldron waggons underneath the staith supports, collecting spilled coal and waste materials. (A.Bowles/Restoration and Archiving Trust)

4.28. Seaham Harbour Dock Co. no.18 was built by Stephen Lewin, a minor engineering foundry at Poole, Dorset. It was supplied to the Londonderry Railway in 1877 as an 0-4-0 well tank. It saw numerous changes to its appearance during its 93 year working life at Seaham. In the early 1900s it was converted to a saddle tank as seen here on the Seaham Harbour Dock Co. staiths. (J.Wiltshire)

4.29. The locomotive arrived at Beamish in 1975 and in 1977 was restored to an approximation of its original appearance and operated on the railway system at the museum. It is seen here at the goods shed in the railway station but in the early 1980s was placed on display in the colliery engine shed.

4.30. The Colliery Yard has been worked by visiting steam locomotives since the revitalising of the railway exhibits in 2005. NCB no.22, an A.Barclay 0-4-0ST their no.2274 of 1949, visited from the Bowes Railway and is shunting chaldrons nos.326 and 528 behind the screens and loading bays. (P.D.Jarman)

4.31. The successors to the chaldron waggons were the NER 10½ ton wagons made to diagram P4, the standard design from then onwards. These were still bottom emptying despite their rectangular shape. Some are being shunted at the colliery screens by another visiting A.Barclay 0-4-0ST. This one is No.3 *Colin McAndrew & Co* AB no.1228 of 1911 from the Chasewater Railway in Staffordshire. (P.D.Jarman)

4.32. If no.1 is an unusual locomotive, then here are two more based on traction engines. *The Blue Circle* is a 2-2-0WT built by Aveling & Porter, no.9449, in 1926 for the cement company. The 4wWT geared version is *Sir Vincent*, Aveling & Porter 8800 of 1917, built for Vickers Armstrong, Erith, Kent and in 1932 sold to BOCM next door. It was preserved at Hollycombe, Liphook, Hampshire, but is privately owned. (P.D.Jarman)

4.33. Out in the country *The Blue Circle* is pulling two of the NER 10½ ton wagons in NCB Bowes livery. The locomotive is based at the Battlefield Line near Market Bosworth. These locomotives were ideal for small shunting yards. The visit was on 3rd September 2010. (P.D.Jarman)

Internal Combustion

4.34. Petrol and diesel locomotives began to be built for shunting in the early 1900s. This is McEwan Pratt patent Petrol Locomotive no.680 of 1916. It was first supplied to Richard Johnson & Nephew Ltd in Bradford. It was later sold to W.R.Jacobs & Co Ltd and used at their Aintree biscuit factory near Liverpool. It was nicknamed 'Jacob' because its resemblance to Jacobs' biscuit tins. It worked there until 1968 when it was presented to Beamish. (B.Webb)

4.35. 'Jacob' was originally fitted with Baguley 60hp petrol engine which was replaced in 1921 by a 40hp White & Poppe petrol engine. Transmission is mechanical. It was stored at the Bahamas Locomotive Society's premises at Dinting, Derbyshire, until 1990. (P.D.Jarman)

4.36. Visiting locomotives have to be negotiated in and out of the museum and this shows the type of low-loading transporter used. This ERF tractor is called The Power and The Glory. It is bringing a very early diesel electric locomotive which had been built locally by Armstrong Whitworth, 0-4-0DE D21 of 1933. It was the first of a range of standard diesel electric shunters. (P.D.Jarman)

4.37. Locomotive no.14 0-4-0DE AW D21 is now standing outside the Beamish Regional Museum Store. Sold to the North Eastern Electric Supply Company, it worked at Dunston generating station until 1973 by which time it had Gardner diesel engine. It was preserved by the Hexham Rolling Stock group in 1975 and went to the National Railway Museum, York, in 1978. Restored there in 2004, it was transferred to Shildon for the opening of 'Locomotion' and came to Beamish in 2008. (P.D.Jarman)

4.38. A very popular diesel mechanical shunting locomotive was the Ruston & Hornsby 88DS 4wDM. Beamish's example is no.476140 built in 1963. Being a relatively modern locomotive, it is usually out of sight when Beamish is open to the public. Here it is receiving some attention in front of the Carr House signal box. It was transferred to the Bowes Railway in 2011. (P.D.Jarman)

Ancillary items

4.39. Harton Coal Company E2 4wWE electric locomotive was built in 1908 by Siemens, no.455, for the Westoe electric coal railway in South Shields. E2 was withdrawn in March 1984 and was then the oldest working electric locomotive on the oldest working electric railway in the country. Saved at the last moment it went to the West Yorkshire Transport Museum until 1989 when it went to the Museum of the Working Horses in Halifax. It was sold to Beamish in March 1991. (R.R.Darsley)

4.40. This robust elephantine machine is a cross between a self-propelled crane and a railway locomotive. It was built by Black, Hawthorn of Gateshead, their no.897, in 1883. It was used in the vast steel works at Consett to move iron and steel billets around the site. Numbered E1, it was the first of a large number of similar 2-4-0CT locomotives. It was converted to oil burning in 1965 and withdrawn in 1975 coming to Beamish in 1978. The photograph was taken in 1893. (V.Dunn/Beamish coll.)

4.41. This 22 ton crane was built by Henry J.Coles Ltd of Derby. It is believed that this is the oldest 'Coles Crane' in existence. Working at the Avonmouth docks of the Port of Bristol Authority from 1917, it was re-purchased by Coles Cranes Ltd in 1978 and renovated to working condition. It was presented to Beamish in 1998 and in May 2002 was displayed near the Tram depot. (R.R.Darsley)

4.42. Beamish has in its collection a number of narrow gauge wagons, including a replica snowplough, based on the remains of an example which operated at Rookhope in Weardale. Narrow gauges are useful and man-sized. Here 2ft gauge 0-4-0ST *Peter Pan* is working on a construction site at the Beamish 'Power of the Past' event. (P.D.Jarman)

4.43. On 16th April 2010, temporary narrow gauge lines were laid near the Mahogany Drift mine. The two visiting locomotives, both of Kerr Stuart's 'Wren' class, were *Peter Pan* 0-4-0ST KS no.4256 of 1922, which came from the Leighton Buzzard Narrow Gauge Railway Society, and 0-4-0ST KS no.3114 of 1918 based at the Vale of Rheidol Railway, Aberystwyth. (P.D.Jarman)

→ 4.44. The Mahogany Drift mine, sunk in 1850 but reopened in 1931 to serve Beamish Second (Chophill) pit, has narrow gauge rail-tracks going into the mine. Sparks from diesel or electric locomotives might ignite gas underground. This could be avoided if the power was compressed air. "Issing Sid" is a replica of a compressed air 0-4-0 locomotive built by the Grange Foundry of Durham in 1880 and used in the Lambton Collieries until the 1900s. The idea caught on overseas, especially in the USA, but not in the UK. (J.Harrop/Beamish coll.)

← 4.45. To end the Colliery section, this is a fine picture of *Twizell*. The locomotive's restoration was carried out at Marley Hill and finished in 2010. This is the inaugural run on passenger service for the Tanfield Railway, double heading with 0-4-0ST *Sir Cecil A.Cochrane* on 9th May 2010. (D.Hewitt)

5. THE POCKERLEY WAGGON WAY

VII Pockerley Waggon Way

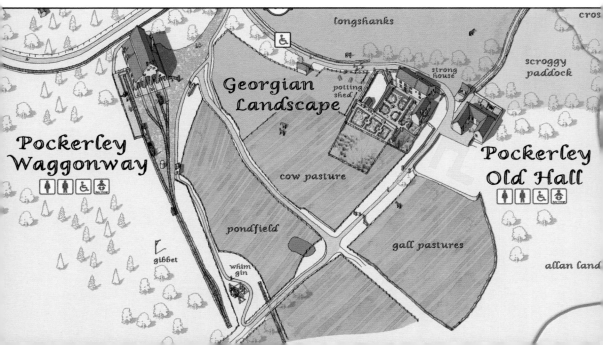

The waggon way emerges

5.1. An overall view of the Pockerley waggon way with the Great Shed and the station platform was taken in August 2000. The Great Shed is modelled on the main building of Timothy Hackworth's Soho Works at Shildon and contains material from Robert Stephenson's Forth Banks Works at Newcastle.

➤ 5.2. This close-up of the weather vane on the Great Shed features *Locomotion* and its train in a stand-off with a cow, as well as the chimney of the replica *Locomotion*. This was the first of the replicas at Beamish, being built by Locomotion Enterprises (1975) Ltd under the guidance of Mike Satow for the 150th Anniversary of the Stockton & Darlington Railway.

5.3. *Locomotion* is hauling a rake of chaldron waggons along the colliery sidings with Pockerley Manor in the background. The replica came to Beamish after the Anniversary event and was regularly demonstrated on the colliery line. In 1995 it was given a major rebuild and moved to the developing Pockerley waggon way.

5.4. This view of the station area on 8th July 2006 shows a train at the platform. The station 'office' is made from an old low pressure steam boiler and in the foreground are the remains of the winding engine from the Warden Law incline on the Hetton Railway. (R.R.Darsley)

5.5. This is *Locomotion* on the train on the waggon way. Next to the locomotive is Hawks, a replica of a 1840s chaldron, which carries an air compressor to power the modern braking required today. Then follows a replica of an S&DR 1829-1831 coach built by Kitching of Darlington and a S&DR 1825 'Tub' or 'Long' coach. The chaldron waggon, Moore, is another replica 1840s chaldron used by the guard. (P.D.Jarman)

5.6. *Locomotion* has travelled widely and featured in many TV and films. Here it is at Peterborough on the Nene Valley Railway in 1993 filming for the 1994 BBC 'Middlemarch' series. Over the winter of 2005/2006 Locomotion received new boiler tubes and a full examination to ensure continued operation well into this decade.

5.7. The Hetton Colliery locomotive led the Stockton & Darlington Railway centenary procession in steam in September 1925 and was presented to the York Railway Museum in July 1926. It was originally thought to be built by George Stephenson in September 1822 and rebuilt by Hetton Coal Co. Ltd in 1853 and again in about 1882. It was being used as a stationary boiler in the saw mill at Hetton Railway workshops before preservation.

5.8. The Hetton locomotive came to Beamish and was examined thoroughly, as it appears to be a mixture of design periods. The conclusion was that it was built by Hetton Colliery in 1852 to an archaic pattern. It is posed with *Locomotion* in the colliery sidings.

The Replicas multiply

5.9. This oil painting was done by an unknown artist in around 1826. It is of *Steam Elephant* at Wallsend. The picture itself has an interesting history but it shows a locomotive built by Hawks & Co., Gateshead, between 1814 and 1815 to the design of a locomotive pioneer William Chapman, and John Buddle, 'King of the Coal Trade' and delivered to Buddle's Wallsend colliery. That is just about all that is known about the locomotive.

5.10. The painting is of such technical accuracy that in the 1990s it provided the base information for building a replica of the locomotive, which was the first locomotive in the world to have a six wheel arrangement. The replica was completed in 2001. This is widely acknowledged as a triumph of research and engineering talent. The building was done by Dorothea Restorations and Alan Keef Ltd.

5.11. *Steam Elephant* is approaching the end of the Pockerley waggon way in this photograph. Pockerley Old Hall and farm are in the background. Besides the locomotive and transport developments of the 1820s, this area of Beamish demonstrates the agricultural and animal husbandry advances of the North East in this period. (J.Harrop/Beamish coll.)

5.12. *Puffing Billy* is currently the newest of the replica locomotives and was built by Alan Keef Ltd in 2006 (their no.71). It is based on the surviving locomotive displayed in the Science Museum, London, and is seen under steam test at Alan Keef's works near Ross-on-Wye. The original was one of at least two locomotives built at Wylam Colliery in 1813/1814. There is some debate as to whether William Hedley or Timothy Hackworth designed the locomotives. (P.D.Jarman)

5.13. From the late 1820s both *Puffing Billy* and its stable mate *Wylam Dilly* (now in the Royal Scottish Museum, Edinburgh) were rebuilt into their present form, which is the form Beamish has chosen to replicate. Both locomotives survived in service until the mid 1800s. The replica arrived at Beamish in 2006. Technically a new locomotive, it had to be fully examined by Her Majesty's Railway Inspectorate before use. *Puffing Billy* is a nickname based on its distinctive 'chuff'. The original was named *Jane* after one of William Hedley's daughters. (A.Coulls)

The horse waggon way

5.14. One of the items launched with *Puffing Billy* at the 'Georgian North' event on 24th May 2006 was a whim gin. This is a horse-powered winding gear for the shaft of a very early coal mine, usually known as a 'bell' pit. Behind is the Great Shed with Locomotion on the waggon way, but this gin takes us back to the age of the wooden waggon way. (R.R.Darsley)

5.15. The horse drawn wooden waggon way is under construction (though the use of modern tools was allowed). In Georgian days, the fencing was with split poles but the waggon way required accurately and expensively sawn wood. Beamish wooden waggon way is laid on stone ballast for improved draining, but this has to be covered for the horse to walk along. (P.D.Jarman)

5.16. Shown on the finished waggon way is a replica Wallsend chaldron waggon of 1815. These carry one chalder and are thus smaller than the Black waggons in earlier pictures. The other replica is of the Throckley Brickworks dandy cart. These were used to convey the horse by train downhill. Gravity moved the heavy loaded waggons, the horse pulling the empty waggons (and its cart) on the return uphill journey. (R.R.Darsley)

5.17. The waggon way is in operation with both chaldrons 45 and 46. The effectiveness of a wooden waggon way over the roads of that time can be judged by the load that one horse could pull on a waggon way would take four to six horses on the road. (P.D.Jarman)

Away from home

5.18. Replicas enable early technology to be demonstrated without compromising or damaging any original artefacts. Sometimes, as with *Steam Elephant*, the artefacts are just not there. They have proved very popular and toured widely. An early venture for *Locomotion* was the 'Gateshead Garden Festival' in 1990 where it trundled along a demonstration track wearing sponsors' badges and with the huge Dunston staiths in the background.

5.19. *Locomotion* went twice to Japan and once to the USA. Wearing a Union Flag, it is parading next to X3985, Union Pacific's mighty Challenger 4-6-6-4, arguably the largest locomotive built. It is preserved in working order by the company that bought it from the American Locomotive Company in 1943. The meeting was Sacramento Steam Fair May 3rd-12th 1991, commemorating the anniversary of the California State Railway Museum. (J.Rees)

5.20. An overseas visit for *Puffing Billy* was to Holland and here it is in the company of 0-6-0T 7853 *Navizence* of the Nederlandse Spoorwagon. Built in 1910, 7853 is based at the Museum Buurt Spoorweg (MBS), Haaksbergen, Overijssd, Holland. The occasion was the 40th anniversary of MBS as a heritage railway held from 27th-28th May 2007. (P.D.Jarman)

5.21. *Puffing Billy* ventured onto Great Western Railway territory at Tyseley, Birmingham, in the company of Castle class 4-6-0 7029, *Clun Castle*, and 4-6-0 4936 *Kinlet Hall*, on 28th-29th June 2008 to celebrate 100 years of the locomotive depot's operation. (P.D.Jarman)

5.22. A visit to Barrow Hill Roundhouse Railway Centre on 22nd August 2008 for 'Rail Power 2008' saw *Puffing Billy* in the presence of C-CDH Western D1023 *Western Fusilier* from the National Railway Museum, York. (P.D.Jarman)

6. A HINT TO THE FUTURE

6.1. The priority for the railway will be the restoration of the NER coaches. There is a prototype for the short train at Beamish shown in this photograph of the North Sunderland Railway taken shortly before closure in 1951. Two NER class Y7 0-4-0T were sold to Pelaw Main Coal Co. in 1931, worked locally and have survived. Look out for no.8088 returning to its native heath to work the Beamish passenger trains. (N.E.Stead coll.)

6.2. This is the state of Gateshead tram no.51 when it was found. It was built in 1901 as double decker no.45 and rebuilt in 1917 as a single deck for the Teams service. Collected in summer 2006, it could be the next project for the Beamish tramway. (P.D.Jarman)

6.3. Gateshead no.51 looked like this when working through to Newcastle. It is in Neville Street near Newcastle Central station. It would be a challenge to return it to this condition. Visiting celebrity trams will continue to appear on special occasions. (G.Hearse/Beamish coll.)

6.4. Similarly the restoration of the Lewin 0-4-0WT no.18 from Seaham Harbour would be a gem in the colliery yard and there is always work to be done on the historic wagon collection. Why not become a Friend of Beamish Museum and join a working party? (R.R.Darsley)

6.5. The restoration of no.1 and the partial restoration of no.17 shows what can be achieved and, while much has been done, there is always something more that can be done to keep the reputation of the museum in the forefront of conservation. (P.D.Jarman)

6.6. The future of working steam at the Station seems assured by the purchase in early 2011 of 0-4-4T *Dunrobin*. Built by Sharp, Stewart & Co. in 1895 this locomotive was the runabout of Highland Railway director, the Duke of Sutherland. Retired in 1948, it was displayed from 1950 alongside the Romney Hythe & Dymchurch Railway at New Romney in Kent. In 1965 a Canadian businessman exported it to Fort Steele, a Canadian version of Beamish. Moves now by Beamish to repatriate it have been successful. In every way it is an ideal Victorian loco for the Museum's operation. (R. Whethman)

MP Middleton Press

EVOLVING THE ULTIMATE RAIL ENCYCLOPEDIA

Easebourne Lane, Midhurst, West Sussex.
GU29 9AZ Tel:01730 813169

www.middletonpress.co.uk   email:info@middletonpress.co.uk
A-978 0 906520   B- 978 1 873793   C- 978 1 901706   D-978 1 904474   E - 978 1 906008

All titles listed below were in print at time of publication - please check current availability by looking at our website - *www.middletonpress.co.uk* or by requesting a Brochure which includes our *LATEST* RAILWAY TITLES also our TRAMWAY, TROLLEYBUS, MILITARY and WATERWAYS series